TOM'S RABBIT

A Surprise on the Way to Antarctica

MEREDITH HOOPER

Illustrated by BERT KITCHEN

NATIONAL GEOGRAPHIC SOCIETY

Washington, D.C.

The story in this book really happened, on a voyage
to Antarctica in 1910. The ship was called the Terra Nova.
Her captain was Robert Scott, and Tom Crean,
the sailor, was a member of the crew.

Tom the Sailor picked up Little Rabbit carefully in his big hands. He wrapped her in an old woolly sweater.

"You need a nest, Little Rabbit," said Tom. "Somewhere on this ship there is just the right place—warm and quiet and cozy. Let's go and find it."

Tom the Sailor looked at the black cat with one white whisker. The ship's cat was tucked up in a warm, cozy place. He lay in his own little hammock, just like the sailors' hammocks, with his own little pillow and blanket.

"This hammock is full of black cat," said Tom. "There's no room for you here, Little Rabbit."

Tom the Sailor looked up at the skylight where the ship's parrot was swinging on her perch.

"Hello, Polly," said Tom.

"Hello, Polly," said the parrot.

"You can't live on a perch, Little Rabbit," said Tom, giving the parrot a piece of string to unravel.

Carefully holding Little Rabbit, Tom the Sailor climbed down the ladder into the ship's hold. There were boxes and sacks and barrels, in stacks and heaps. It was very cold.

Tom peered around and shivered. "It's much too cold and dark down here for you, Little Rabbit," he said, and climbed back up again quickly.

In the big cabin, everyone was busy hanging up paper lanterns, paper chains, and flags.

"Come and help us put up the decorations!" they called. "Come on, Tom."

"Not now," said Tom. "I have to find a nest for my rabbit."

Good smells were coming from the galley. Tom looked
around the door. The cook was stirring something in
a big saucepan.

"What's for dinner?" asked Tom.

"Special surprises for a special dinner," said the cook.
"You just wait and see."

Tom the Sailor put on his big, warm jacket. He pulled
on his woolly hat and woolly gloves.

"We're going up on deck, Little Rabbit," said Tom.
"Mind now, keep warm!"

Snow was falling gently. The sea was covered in big pieces of ice like white meringue. Icebergs floated slowly by, like spiky mountains.

Two whales lifted their great backs in a patch of blue-black water, then sank below the surface.

Fat, silvery seals lay on the ice, yawning and scratching themselves with their flippers. A little group of penguins stood staring at the ship. More penguins scurried across the ice in a long line. One penguin climbed to the top of an ice hill and the others pushed him off.

The deck was filled with dogs. Brown dogs, hairy dogs, black dogs, and yellow dogs with pointy ears and curly tails.

Tom tucked Little Rabbit deep inside his jacket.

"Hello, dogs!" said Tom. The dogs barked and yelped and howled.

High above the deck, up against the sky, a wooden barrel was lashed to the mast. Pure white birds flew round and round the rigging.

"It's no good going up there with you, Little Rabbit," said Tom. "You can't climb, and you can't fly."

Tom the Sailor went forward to the place where the ponies were kept in strong wooden stalls. The ponies banged at the sides of their stalls with their sharp hooves.

"This ship is full up," said Tom, "it's crowded with animals. Where can I find you a warm, quiet, cozy place for your nest, Little Rabbit?"

Little Rabbit's long, silky ears drooped.

"I've got it!" shouted Tom suddenly. He ran down eight steps, and poked his head into a gap under the deck where the hay for the ponies was stored. The air smelt sweet.

"Just the place for a nest!" said Tom. Carefully he unwrapped Little Rabbit from the old woolly sweater, and put her on to the hay. Little Rabbit hopped around, sniffed the hay, and lay down.

"And now," said Tom happily, "it's time for my Christmas dinner!"

Everyone sat down around the long table in the big cabin.
They ate . . .

Tomato Soup,
Roast Mutton,
Plum Pudding,
Mince Pies.

Then they opened little parcels from their families.
They played games, and sang songs. They were a very long
way away from home, but it was a good Christmas party.

When it was nearly bedtime, Tom went to see if Little Rabbit was all right.

He poked his head into the gap under the deck where the hay was stored. Little Rabbit lay in her warm, cozy nest in the hay. Lying next to her were seventeen baby rabbits.

"That's the best Christmas present ever!" said Tom, happily. "Seventeen babies! Now I can give a rabbit to each of my friends. Well, nearly!"

And he stroked Little Rabbit's long, silky ears.

Tom looked around at the night. The deck was covered in glittering snow. The world was utterly quiet and still. The sun was a soft golden ball, and the ice glowed white, with purple shadows.

"Merry Christmas," said Tom to the world.

The great white continent of Antarctica is surrounded by ice-covered seas.
On Christmas Day, 1910, the Terra Nova was pushing through the ice, toward
land. The men on board, led by Captain Scott, hoped to be the first people to
reach the South Pole. Their husky dogs and ponies would help pull sledges loaded
with food, tents, and sleeping bags across the frozen snow. Little Rabbit was one
of many pets on board.

Tom Crean got close to the South Pole before turning back and helping to save
the life of another explorer. Captain Scott, with four companions, did reach
the Pole, only to find that a Norwegian expedition led by Roald Amundsen had
arrived before them.